What the Sky Lacks

0 3 JUL 2019

What the Sky Lacks

Poems by
Thom Caraway

Korrektiv Press

Spokane ✳ New Orleans
Copenhagen

For permissions and ordering information visit:
www.korrektivpress.com

Managing Editor and Designer: Jeffrey G. Dodd

First Edition

ISBN: 9780983151357

Contents

Weather, which is only a nuisance in the city,
takes on the power of the gods here,
and vast cycles of climate make all man's
successes momentary and ambiguous.

Thomas McGrath

Eastbound on the Empire Builder

You see the backs of buildings,
yellow-lit loading docks, heavy men
slogging pallets at 1 a.m. Warehouse bars
and industrial parks, brick stacks
shouting steam at low skies.
Fork-lift drivers load trucks
with tomorrow's commerce.
You pass whole cities of ruined cars
and scrap iron, an empire of delivery trucks.
What a strange congress they make.
The culvert under I-90 has been dry for years
and still the trains whistle past.

And I am bound east,
soon for the twisting wind of North Dakota,
where these men have never been,
but dream of in their dreams of
uninterrupted sky. A world built
of unknown language. When they wake,
they look for the low mountains
surrounding Spokane, know that some
terrible landscape lies beyond.

When Richard Dreyfuss Said
"This is Important," He Meant It

A stop sign crazy-dances in January wind,
like that scene in *Close Encounters of the Third Kind*,
Richard Dreyfuss about to be burned
by the light of the alien craft.

If only it were that easy.

To look up, hand shading my eyes,
into the face of something unknown,
beautiful enough to scorch itself
into the skin of my face.

We'd all wander around, branded
by our various alien beauties—
a long winter idling at last into warmth,
crystal sagebrush under winter sun.

When we meet, we'll smile privately at the grandeur
of our little zealotries, and, unable to look
directly at one another, nod knowingly,
I, too, have seen something.

An Unfinished Sky

The clouds are not afraid
of this soft death, this
falling apart—first a finger,
then whatever else your ailment chooses.
The clouds fall back to earth,
little explosions in the autumn soil,
but even the rain will kill you now,
the black business of business,
hiding in shadows that make trout toxic.
The *Washington Fishing Regulations* ask women
of child-bearing age to please not eat more
than one fish per year from the Upper Spokane River,
and further, young men, please, do not go on.
Your farm-raised fish are sterile.
Climb no peaks you have not named.
Stop feeling the wind as you set your camp,
the ground is uneven, and you will never find peace
in this hour before darkness.

A Good Season Ends

After little league games, we'd play
like small men in the fields
behind Maria's Pizza. It was the last game
of the season; we'd done well and nobody
wanted to leave, though we didn't know why.
Bobby Danielson was impossibly tall,
and he led us through the fields.

I stopped for no reason, like boys do,
and found myself in dark weeds, running
my hands over the tops of the tall stalks,
rough like a long span of highway
bending toward Montana. Ahead
in the shrinking light: voices of the boys
I loved. Still so far ahead.

At the Parkman Bar

Harold Big Lake wins the weekly bar lottery,
and buys shots of Cuervo for the six other patrons.
Richard Yellowbird owns the place,
a run-down trailer in a post-office town.
He hangs eight-by-ten black-and-whites
of all the regulars and longtime residents.
Makes it feel busy, he says. *They're always here.*
Harold just got his second DUI
and tries to stay away from Billings.
Harold's brother has been stretching
barbed-wire at the x-bar ranch
but hasn't been paid. If there's no money
tomorrow, he'll quit, maybe see if a ranch
further down the road needs hands.

I have no cash, so Harold buys me a beer.
I sit and listen to stories of bored Crow,
as though my small pain was a part of theirs.
I miss my girls, I say.
He buys me another, says,
Welcome to Parkman.

The Dream of the Wrecker

*...darkness will know him when it blooms and becomes
the world.*
        —Christopher Howell

He dreams of children flying apart in a sunburst,
or drowning in bare inches of water.
Everyone he loved is gone and the clouds
will not end. He tries to work with solder,
fuse broken things to whole ones,
wedding veils to funeral shrouds.

He will become in the name of God and vengeance,
an instrument of pure light, a circular machine
of illumination, sorry for nothing he's done.
The world he knew was once clean
and slow. A place for the elderly and dying.
Down the long arm of a gun

too necessary for careful aim or trivial concessions,
he finds the will of God. And it has little to do
with faith or love. He is sure of that now,
and goes to the place he grew
to love the sounds of people moving in the world,
and he'll be damned if he has to kowtow

to innocence, and the like. In another dream
he finds solace in rusted-out cars.
Women he never knew call him by name,
gather close to crowd out the stars
that are coming from behind the clouds.
They are the same clouds, everything's the same.

Sudden Light at the Crazy Woman Saloon

I am the sheriff of all Wyoming.
I am big bear. Call me *fire.*
Twisted carcass of tree and root.
Orange sky rains wheat.
Ten round bales behind the elk fence
at Amsden Creek. The cragged face
of the rancher at the bar as he opens
and closes his mouth. His daughter
is gone eleven years, his wife gone
five. A mountain lion has been
killing his sheep all year,
but he has a plan. I am the sheriff
of all the West.

How to Hunt Badly

1
Spend most of your life not hunting or even thinking about hunting. Then, marry a small-town girl, who will be a much better shot than you.

2
Be a poor shot. It is best to be even a little afraid of shooting. This will cause you to flinch in the instant before you pull the trigger, anticipating the violence of the kick, or the unfolding of the bullet as it penetrates the body of the animal, the shredding of organs and tissue.

3
Write this poem while hunting. Yes, you're in perfect position, a rocky overlook in the embrace of two drainages. There is sweet mountain grass still green all around you, a brook still running, the kind of place all the books said elk should want to be. The sun has come out to backlight the yellowed tamarack on the hillside opposite and you haven't seen another hunter all morning. Still, there is this poem to write.

4
Have not spoken with your father in twelve years and spend the morning thinking of all the ways you've grown more like him, in appearance and disappearance.

5
Or, have spoken to your father just last week, and remember that you're still afraid of him, his looming temper, like when you were a boy.

6
Still be that boy.

7

Say prayers you know will go unanswered. Say prayers for the glorious elk of the Blue Mountains, and know that even were you to see one, legal and within range, it is most likely that you wouldn't pull the trigger.

8

Hunt in the vicinity of fierce men running chainsaws all morning. Say nothing to them. They are a half-dozen fathers.

9

Think about your wife, three hours away, and sad these last many years. Neither of you know why, but you know there's little you can do.

10

Get up from your spot and leave, the moment you know you shouldn't. There are shots further down the drainage, and across the ridge behind you. Know that every elk in the Wenaha-Tucannon herd, every silver-tipped seven-by-seven bull, every cow and calf, every ghost-footed spike elk there ever was is converging on your position. You hear the thunder of their hooves shaking the mountain beneath you. Get up at that moment. Flee.

Field Dressing

The buck hunched over his wound
like it was the last edible scrub sage
for three hundred miles, then shot straight
up a hillside, punctured heart pumping
blood wherever it could.

Sharpen the knife to surgical precision, then
slide it between the skin and the organ sac.
Remove the organs all at once. Be gentle.
You must reach with both
cold hands into the rough cavern.
Feel the spent life, and lift the organs.
Lift and pull, as though bringing the first
life of the world into the glaring light of day.

Naming the Spiders

In one of the pictures you gave me, I am four years old. Your hands were gods of love and cooking, as big as the whole mountain. You pulled the stinger from my foot when I stepped on a bee—even showed me the bee close up, the cilia of its abdomen in the ridges of your palm.

When the weather starts to turn this year, and warm wind rumors spring, I will help you plant your annuals. You will tell me the names of everything we put in the ground, Latin and common. I'll dig in the thawing soil, fingers against the small rocks as I shape the holes just so, like you showed me, years ago. Half of everything you buy, you will give to me to take home for my yard. We'll pull straw from the perennials, and you will have me dig some up, *just to make some space*, but really, you want me to have them, too. Everything of yours becomes mine this way. Old books. Christmas ornaments. All your family pictures. Your painting of Pine Mountain after it burned in the dusty summer of '78. We left for Spokane soon after, leaving behind the nighttime trips to the creek for fresh water, moon guiding our way, you pointing out the stars with the best stories. When you give me the rose bush by your back door, give me the spiders too—you could not name them, but I want them just the same.

A Visitor's Guide to North Dakota

1
Potato stink and cloud sweat. The wind can turn, they say
as quick as your mind, but never mind that.

Instead, watch river height and creek run,
water can rise and wash away towns.

Meanwhile, lakes are high, or low, catfish and carp
lurk on muddy bottoms. A man stands in a slow river,
casts again and again. His line brands
the still surface of the water, but no fish rise.

2
The maps have no language
for topography, elevation
is measured in years.

In October, the trees are charcoal
drawings, dusty black fading gray.
Men move slow,

heads down, bowed to wind,
to the flat horizon
stretched like a lifeline
across an empty sky.

3
Devil's Lake swallows whole forests,
an army of skeleton birch in shallow water,
waves spilling onto the highway
when the wind picks up. The argument is
cut a channel to the river,
or let it take the road.
Garrison Dam broke the Missouri

and drowned three towns.
Let the highway go.

   4
Sky illustrates the old man's face.
His mouth is working on something. His bus
has passed. It is four degrees. Wind pushes leaves
past his ankles. On the slow plod home,
he considers the dogs in the alley.
He remembers nights in bars, the women he knew.
The scotch will taste good tonight.
All the old dreams fade.
The dogs will die of cold. Soon enough,
the Scotch won't help his shaking hands.

   5
Then it is winter.
Snow falls deep on unwalked trails.
Follow rabbits
to food and water. Dim sound
of retreating footsteps. Remember August—
such heat. Your eyes
are much colder now. Make fire
or die. That's how it is here. North Dakota
is no place for thin blood. Look for shelter belts,
find relief from unending wind.

Certain Knowledge

Morning sounds after long night.
The cold sun and I am frightened.
One vast universe, and nothing in it
but me. Not the noise the sun makes
but the silence. Where have you gone?
Across the river, three men
put a boat in water,
each of them still-lifed
as cars pass on the Point Bridge.
Fishing poles describe long arcs
through morning-thick air.

Yesterday I loved you—
your face blurred with stars.

We share space, as close
as we can be, but all joining
is illusion, light.

From the just-harvested fields
of western Minnesota, the night sky—
a riot of stars and satellites. Mars as close
now as anything that large ever gets.
Somewhere in the long dark
Pioneer 10 reflects the last light
of a day we've already seen
as it pushes ever further, revealing
the edge of what we know for certain.

Language Acquisition

Words become fuzzy; I translate
from western to plains. *Mountain*
is *butte. River* is *river,* but not.
Tree is *drowned. Cold: not bad.*
Unspeakable: cold.

Emma puts words together,
names her world with syllables.
Deep in night, she wakes,
forms sounds, and comes to make them to me.

One arm asleep, I pull her into bed, lay her between
her mother and me. I whisper *forest,* and she laughs.
I whisper *elevation,* and she says, *oogla.*
I whisper *home,* and she whispers *home.*

Her head rests in the bend of my arm,
small breath warm against my skin,
as she blinks her way back to sleep.
I don't know what woke her,
will never know the dreams
of her unformed language,
but when she sleeps here,
dreams until morning in the shelter
of her parents' bodies,
she makes no noise at all.

North Dakota

I feel it through my skin   there
its words are my words
its shape is the shape of my hands
its light the light of my
it disappears in shadow
like trees   like sky

it's everywhere   it does not
let me dream
its people in the full light of sky
drown the sun
make me ache   laugh and ache
speak though I lack the strength

Solitude Like the Moon's

The only boat that goes home
has left. You stand waiting.
Another boat passes, but it knows
only the moon. Moon of six million stars,
of silence and tides. You wait
for your own moon-boat—old worries
in one hand, spare shoes in the other.
You crouch to jump into the space
between one day and everything
that follows.

Look up the river—
winter-killed leaves of oak
and chestnut float past.
From the other direction, a man
poles his long flat boat.
His eyes closed in prayer,
he never sees you.

Then Snow

Whiteout blizzard, a storm
with a name. Sound amplified,
muffled, echoed.
A train in the distance,
steel on steel sings, keens
around the banked corner track
then the accordion crash
as it slows, one car rams
the next, couplings tested
and found secure once more.

Red lights and bells stop,
the arms of the gate rise,
point back to low sky.
Snow across empty tracks
and the tender does slow work—
shuttles empty freight cars
down one track, gas tankers
down another, back and forth
in darkness, back
and forth all night.

Wind wrings snow
from an empty sky,
light snow pulled
off the ground, blown
around until you are not sure
if it is falling
or rising.

ж   ж   ж

My heart jubilates
for those who live
in dangerous places,
where if you are not careful,
the soft snow
will pull you down,
kiss the warmth
from your body,
and allow you sleep.

Closing the Blue Spark

Crickets are the color of asphalt. A train rattles glasses on the bar. The sun dies in the western sky. Whiskey shots, long hair. His hand moves up her thigh. *I'll have another.* Her muzzy voice hangs in murky air. Outside, trees are stripped of leaves. The ground crackles. Somewhere, a sapling Russian Olive gnarls into shape. At the bar, she holds her breath, pushes her hair back from her eyes. Smiles. Dogs run across the tracks. The man and woman stumble into night-weather. The wind howls— advisory in effect until three a.m., central time. Empty store windows reflect light off pavement. Two lovers grope home, knowing the wind will   knowing the night will end soon enough. Beds give no comfort to those going home so late. They find their way around: new bodies, old motions. Sometime past sleep, she pushes his arm from her naked hip, rises from bed and dresses. Returns again to windblown night.

What the Sky Lacks

The skies I've known—
sheared against mountains
so that the puzzle is not where sky ends
and land begins, but can I touch it
from Mica Peak or Diamond Head.
But the Dakota sky billows.
I've been told about this sky,
piled high all around, no escape,
no horizon. But horizon
is what the mountains define,
what the sun sets behind.
What is there to aspire to
if nothing approaches the sun?
How else to know I am home
until Mt. Spokane appears
in the west, a pole star, constant,
bare granite upper slopes giving way
to pine and fir? When the sky allows,
the weather station sparkles, high above
Kirk's Lodge, and the road climbs,
past Pennsylvanian time, through Mississippian,
Devonian, and Ordovician time to arrive
shining at last among rocks formed
in the first hours of the Earth.
  And there, the sky does the slow work
of erasing.

Where the Trees Begin, Where the Trees End

The people on the train
all say how much they love
the train. A man boards in Red Wing,
says he wishes he had more children
and that they lived further away.
He walks into cold wind at Minot.

Old scars twitch and glimmer
in the hills east to west. Tracks parallel
Highway 2. The train: hollow
and fast, rush and chunk of steel
over thick oiled ties and banked gravel right-of-way.

As we spoke on the phone,
my son held a tongue depressor
behind his teeth to separate the top
from the bottom, his newest speech-
therapy exercise. *I can't touch it,*
he said, *with my tongue.*
He is remaking the shapes
his mouth makes, a new language
emerging. Tongue to the roof
of the mouth, to the bottom.
'T' sounds become hard 'C's.

We take our time
on the phone. He asks me if,
when I visit, we can use
the telescope I sent last year.
Maybe we could play chess, too.

In central Montana, past Shelby,
abruptly, trees. Trees by the millions,

spreading in every direction.
Not the truncated shelterbelts—
gnarly cottonwoods, dead-bleached birch—
of the northern plains.
Into Glacier, it's Grand and Doug Fir,
an army of wide spruce and Lodgepole.
Down Marias Pass, the snow falls heavy,
ten feet as we pass the Izaak Walton, and an engine
fitted with a beak-nosed plow moves slow,
clearing tracks and side-tracks.

But I notice all of this later, when
I'm off the train, and suddenly back on the rich,
dark, frozen soil of North Dakota, the tracks
rewound, the trees again behind. Time passes
more slowly here, the present reaches further back
and further forward, is without horizon.
In the present of arrival, I don't remember
the past as the past, as if I was moved here
by sleight of hand, as if in all the hours
of clanking along the rails
I had slept, or dreamt, or died
only to be born again in the distant present,
my son's wild treed world far behind.
This another place, a new shape
forming in my mouth.

The Wrecker Sees Snow and Thinks of Home

The great fires of youth
have died. The slow decay of wood
and bone remains. I tire
of too much sky, too little
heat and white clouds.
When does time turn?
Now is the season for storm
and fire. On the television—
spying and shooting, bombs,
and I think: *more.*
Extinction is the only way home.
There are no white flowers
of innocence or love. We are the swift
hollow voice of metal on metal.

The universe is created each time
I close or open my eyes, swing my axe.
Maybe the universe will implode
after stretching so far that all
that remains is to fold inexorably back
to where it began, a pin point, a fixed center
where everything, and nothing, is true.

Grandma Weatherby, Come to Speak her Mind

The fare was sumptuous. The turkey had brined for twenty-four hours, the oven preheated to 375, the door duct-taped shut. Potatoes were mashed, mixed with cream, butter, salt, pepper, garlic, and parmesan cheese. Dishes in the second oven: enough food to burn down a house. And at 12:37 in the afternoon, Grandma Weatherby knocked twice and let herself in. First, the animals ran for cover. Two napkins spontaneously combusted. Grandma Weatherby asked for a glass of wine. Gary, of course, filled a glass for her. "Oh, too much, dear." Her boyfriend, Owen, wearing a black bolo tie and black vest, nodded gravely. Grandma Weatherby hadn't been invited, and the location of the dinner had been kept under tight wraps. "Your hair is beyond reproach, Jane. Gary, still employed?" Her dress began to change color and her hair sizzled. Owen continued to nod. Four children spontaneously combusted. "I'll thank you for not inviting me, and for keeping the location of the dinner under tight wraps. I've come to speak my mind." The children of her children removed dishes from the oven. The turkey was carved, the ham sliced. Rolls buttered, plates filled. Meanwhile, Grandma Weatherby spoke her mind. Everything set on the table. Her four previous husbands dead. Afterward, the children were put to bed and the fires went out. And Owen, Owen.

December 1, 20°, Low Skies, Chance of Flurries

Give me snow. Give me drifts
up to my eyes. Forty days and nights.
I want snowplows snowed in, snow days
for every school in North Dakota.
In the vast unbroken silence, we can be saved,
crushed. The sky is not enough.
Snow to obliterate this known world,
to redeem us, make us humble
and dumb, a blizzarded garden.
I don't want to be able to name
any feature the snow covers.

My daughter will toddle out, blink into the sun-
dazzle, and know that this is a world she can
re-create, a world unsullied by names
or knowledge. If she looks at a tree
breaking through the snow and says *la-ga,*
then la-ga is what it shall be. So bury us.
We'll rename the world.

Failure of Imagination

There is much falling
still
to do.

If you find apples
know that I was
a noisy toad in the static electricity
of your youth.

Coming upon a man in water,
your eyes are
logs—dammed, drowned.

Terrible sky
knows no/defines no boundaries
to contain our oceanic dream of ice.

Seek shelter/seek shelter—

Owen is coming home
tonight

from his private war

following his dick
to you.

Become soft red squirrels.

There is cold comfort in turning
inward, squirrel. The gate rusts
on its hinges, same as God.
Come in,
come in—

the couch is still available
in the hotel of   in the casket of
my imagination—
    the rest is noise.

The origin of your question is fire.
The drimmely pop of shotguns
tells birds
be food or feathers.

I never said that—

You are going to—
accosted by your drunk—
but you are   likely   .

In this ancient kiss of shoulder and mountain,
be sure.

The plastic bag you carried your food
home in blows toward Minnesota
or safety.   The trees are frightened
                                            naked.
Running for your life
was never an option.

Store food for winter.
Store food for noise.

Coming up on your left
a man with no mustache—

he looks for blood
under your skin—
take matters   your own hands.

The Last Remaining Light

I've known mountains. I dream them. Light through leaves. Snow in shadows. Specklelight. October cold. Shadowsnow. But it's a trick of air. Tricky sky full of questions. Mountains against sky. Here is where the rain fell, here is where the deer walk to water. Rabbithole my questions. Eat my questions. The coming night is for dying. Savior Creek runs downhill. This I know. Through elk pastures & cow pastures, a wet sliver working into the flesh of Spokane County. It is leaving me. What do I say when an entire mountain leaves me? Two peaks rise into shallow sky, Spokane and Kit Carson. I know names. The Blanchard shoulder-ridge. I walked it, cold & wet, nearing dark. Pound a door, *anyonehome?* Savior Creek, crusted with my *don'tknowwherelam,* frozen over flat ground. This is where the deer bed down. Notice the grass, waist-high in places, but pushed down. Wait for the deer, wait for the kill. But I was lost there. There is no sky without the mountains. Mountains are leaving me. All that remains is sky. Vast feeblememory, a long creek bearing west, toward town.

What Was Once Comfort

I know I can come home, become lost
in the lush territory of your twining legs—
Pacific swell of hip and breast.
There is no pattern for heartbreak
we have not revealed
in the time of our common landscape.
I feel the needle enter your spine,
your writhing fire.

I know I can come home,
find in the heart of winter
some small warmth of my own,
wrap it tight in the space between desire
and muscle. If this is to be our infirmity,
our treatment—
I am ready.
Once, when we were younger,
we knew the insides of our bodies.

When the doctors said cancer
I thought they meant me.
I am certain of so little.
Rivers flow the wrong direction,
Ursa Major too low in the winter sky—
but I hear the crows outside
our bedroom window,
calling to each other
in the early dark
of morning, warning
and greeting.

A Siege of Cranes
with Jennifer Reid

I'm secret with embraces. Soft
murky sod struggles against tyrant rain.
Come with me to the river—we'll leave
the rusting world away. Hands-tied and blind
we keep pronouncing our words of faithloss,
intent on kissing the awful warmth
from our bodies.

End/Beginning

I

Walk with me:
cars move too fast.
Speed and recognition mean nothing
without detail.
      Your walls
      your roofs are no shelter.

Trees in the lake
              dead and grey
but full of birds. The center
of the continent, a pile of stones,
   untouched
by the push and pull of tides.

Walk with me now—
these towns are dying and dead,
but something must be saved,
some shape that absence
has not yet claimed—
knowledge too pure
to utter aloud. Some
deep buried thing
      that will not be shaken free.

The horn has blown, the walls
collapsed—
      this is not a land one survives
on faith alone
     whatever
         your faith is in.

The weather report says *catastrophic*,
but it is worse—wind across snow,
dust of snow falling and rising,

sideways and down, a landscape
of blurred roads and hunkerdown.

   2
Then morning of knowledge,
stretched echoes of echoes,
drifts three feet or more.
Sun off the snow.
Nothing is settled, but from here
we can find our way.

The Wrecker Seeks Guidance
in an Unplowed Field

In our weakness
we have failed.
Renew us,
that we may follow.
The days are surely coming—
it will not be like the broken
covenant of our ancestors,
but I will put my law within them,
and I will write it on their hearts.
I will forgive iniquity, remember sin
no more. Find secret truth. Make me
hear joy and gladness. Create in me
a clean heart, one forged from glass.

The hour has come, I tell you,
unless a grain of wheat falls to the earth and dies.

A Poem for Lisa

A poem for you will have
square corners and a perfect
centered circle. It will have
dark hair, pulled back and tied
up each morning.
It will, if written by someone
else, not know the things
you don't want known,
the blurring faces of old lovers.
A poem for you hides
behind grain bins for a quick smoke,
always just out of sight,
the hill beyond the hill,
the road narrowing and gone
past the silo. You are unafraid
of the cold, but still cold.
There is something in the neat
circle of your life, something
breathing and warm, yours,
not about you, but all
shy-eyed women, all the hidden
voices of the world, as yet silent,
as yet breathing.

When I Could, and then Couldn't, and then the Moon

I hear them as distance. Ears ringing.
Voices in smoke. Trees bare and the creek
unburgeoned by runoff. Damp earth
and leaf. Ground crack, un-ice.
Winter-dead branches we burn for fuel.
We come to the fire in threes,
something solid in the cold shape
of spring. Ringing. I cannot hear.
Soon, no light. I still see
their shapes in the dark, familiar
and haze, beautiful notmine
their voices ringing the fire.
Smoke and wind. Then—orange, low
moon, troubled behind clouds. Me,
the distance the horizon
clouded and alive
unable to see, finally,
what may or may not be there.

Under Sheltering Trees, My Daughter and I Consider the Coming Storm

A full moon glows trees yellow,
dies behind silvering clouds
and my arms become sand.

Things in the yard:
    —a suspicious cat
    —a bouncy ball Emma left behind as the skies
        exclaimed their pregnancy
    —grass unmowed for weeks.

Tympanic concussions from the tin shed
and anxious wind skins the skinny oak—
clearly, the world is ending.
But the dancing cat barks
to the soft ball, *Hooray!*
for now is the time before time ends!
I pick grains of myself
from the planter-box and Emma says,
It's not time for bed.
The dancing cat dances catly.
Emma says, *Yes.*

And there in the rain
the cat, my daughter,
the planter boxes, the flowers
and the long grass, the skies
of full darkness and full rain-ness,
the shingles, the branches of trees,
the sidewalk and the cracks in the sidewalk,
the streets and their lights raise together their arms,
their arms and their tiny yellow voices.

Hunting the Mitchell Property

There is more here
than I expected. Mud from fallow fields
cakes thick, my boots clay-heavy
as I stalk the Park River,
slough and slurry of irrigation
and drainage channels. The deer are thick,
scat and rub, shed antler velvet like moss
on the low choke-cherry.
Cross the river at the bone-bleached
deadfall. Once, a wagon broke down
or a man said, *here.* Homesteads
mushroomed. How much of survival is luck?

The noon whistle at Hoople,
another at Crystal. Men and women
shuffle out, suffer the day,
smoke-break and lunch pail.

Where the river crosses under County 12,
the beavers make their dams
and Dick Mitchell unmakes them,
shovel and shotgun, to keep
his basement from flooding.

In one field, three does browse
scrap corn cobs, a poached buck
thirty feet away, the hunter long gone.
Feast for fox and crow.
Another field horseshoes
an old homestead, timbers
collapsed, but the roof intact.

Near the deadfall, a blue heron
wobbles overhead, long wings crush air.

Come summer, that field will be corn,
and on quiet nights, when the crickets die down,
you will hear the language of corn,
and other prayers for sustenance.

Unexpected Ascendance
in Williston, North Dakota

North Dakota inspires
many things—despair,
alcoholism, mythology.
The Rockies unleash
tide after tide of towering
cumulus, that soar twenty
thousand feet over the earth,
but still reach down
to wet the Dakota soil, to strip
fall trees of leaves in hours.

You'll hear stories
about North Dakota,
but this is my favorite,
because I saw it.
The first eastbound stop in stolid NoDak
is Williston. Puddles from leftover rain—
the ground can only take so much.
A boy on his way home
from an uncle's in Browning.
He's been listening to stories
all day in the observation car—
men from New York, men from London,
a girl from anywhere. The boy detrains,
walks his bag toward his waiting parents.
They greet him. I'd like to say
they smiled, but you know Williston.

He drops his bag and turns
toward the train, makes a run for it.
And this is the part I like: a puddle
between him and the train,
moisture from twenty thousand feet,

rain with more stories than he can imagine,
rain from Montana, from Seattle, from Hong Kong,
from anywhere but Williston, North Dakota.
The boy leaps the puddle. The ease of youth.
And like sometimes happens in my dreams,
he keeps right on going. Up and over
the train, twenty feet, and up and up and up.
His X to Y ratio, with its sudden and stupendous
rate of climb boggles the mind.

Not even in my dreams
do I escape so quickly.
None of my awkward dream-struggling
to master the nuances of thermals or gusts.
The kid is gone in a flash, as quickly
out of North Dakota as a storm,
and who knows when or where
or even if he'll come back down.

On the Westbound Train

500 miles out of Chicago,
a woman slumps in her seat.
Her daughter chitters and screams
and settles down. The first small
rises in the long plains of the Midwest
appear to the north, long table rocks
and plateaus, then the prefatory
mountains of the Continental Divide.
The daughter looks out the window,
Is that a volcano? The mother rises
to the window, searches the horizon.
No, those are just mountains. She pulls
a blanket up. Her left hand grips the edge,
her scarred left hand, puckered and twisted,
as though by fire. Staring out the window now,
she breaks the earth's mantle and magma rises
into the ancient cones and lava tubes
that formed this land, pushing against
the thin sides of brittle granite peaks.
Steam first, then great gouts of lava.
She says again, *Just mountains.*
Her left hand squeezes and flexes,
her fingers straining against the scars
of her first fire. She still feels the inviting
heat as she stared into the flames,
reached in, and took out some small fire for her own.

The Names of Things We've Lost

Shoulder deep in berry bushes,
the trail is hard to see. Hiking Montana
means bears. It's best to make noise—
shout or whistle, carry bells. We shout, *Hey bear,*
we shout, *don't eat us,* or *eat someone else.*
Approaching Stoney Indian Pass, we meet a man
shouting, *Chloe.* Over and over again. *Chloe.*
I make a dumb joke, ask, *Have you lost someone?*
Once, he says.

Walking the continental divide isn't easy.
You have to get there. People collapse
over Swiftcurrent Pass. The trail seems
etched on stone, impossible switchbacks
down a rough cliff, over rivers
and into the valley at last. The heat,
the wind. At some point you're alone
on the trail with nothing
but time, wind, and sun. Trees,
and the noise you make
to keep the thought of bears away.

After Stoney Indian, I think about the things I've lost.
My wallet. Poems. A Tonka bulldozer left too near
the garbage cans when I was five. Joes. Kristas.
Nine years of my son's life. Of the things I do well,
I'm best at absence.

At the end of the valley, some are finished,
the long trail too close to the sky to go on.
But many of us are still out there,
wandering the Highline Trail, the Northern Loop,
stuck under Cathedral Peak in the brief lee
of a blown-down storm shelter,
shouting into empty canyons,
the names of things we've lost.

What the Sky Lacks

Sky and land blurred,
slurred together, gray-earth
gray-sky. The storm has been
coming for days, clouds piled
at the base of the Rockies,
billowing out over Montana,
then released at last
and the march over the plains
lightning like flash bulbs,
popping every second and the thunder
can be heard for days.
This is joy, this vast knowing. You remember
old horizons, the jagged teeth.
Here, you see the earth change
as it changes, the whole glorious pattern
laid bare—watch for days as the first
Arctic system approaches out of the north.

Once More, the Red River

It never seems to stop,
the river. Rising and more rain
then snow, freeze, thaw—
and something
must hold it back. Our weight
is sand and stone. Day
night. Rhythmic swing
arms and arms
stack the bags
stack the bags
sand and stone.
Our weight against the river.
What meager work we do
is twenty miles and ten years long.
Finish and sigh
and the river comes again.
We work another
two feet onto the wall,
for that is what is needed.

On Rivers and Not Dying

From the air, I like guessing
locations by the minute wrinkles
in the landscape as we slide west.
Rivers are the real clues—
and when we land, I try to find them
on maps, to see how close I'd been
to right. Tracing the course of the Madison,
or the Missouri, I think, Yes, I saw that bend.
It was from 36,000 feet, but I am sure
that was the one. Had Lani died of cancer,
I imagine future relationships
would be similar. This is her hip.
It feels right. Something is off.
I like to think that at some point
I would have simply given up,
admired them as I do the rivers,
sinuous and beautiful,
even from a great distance.

The Roadside Nothing Vendor

He has no fruit to sell, no one dollar
videos. Under his summer umbrella,
he sits in an aluminum folding chair.
His sign says nothing, and people stop,
expecting nothing. He has no novels,
no trinkets or post cards. And also none
of the following: light bulbs, boxes,
trips to exotic lands, scrap lumber.
He has no cars to sell, no electric
razors, no seashells, no comic books.
He has no secrets to sell you, no gossip.
The old lady down the road, walking her cat
in a baby stroller—he sells her nothing
as she walks past. The light turns green
and cars go by. He waves and smiles.

Last Wild

"The Bunny Hills" are what the local
kids always called it. There are no
bunnies. The ghosts of the rail-yard
it once was remain. The 30-foot piling,
Devil's Chair, once held the bridge
across the river. Billy's house
down the block, high and long,
was the slaughter-house,
hogs and cattle brought in
by boxcar. Over time, the lines
shifted to the south bank,
the bridge dismantled, and the ties
removed. What remained was earth
and stone, rail spikes and oil barrels.
For years, the kids of West Central
rode bikes and caught snakes there,
the bunny hills, thirty square blocks
of detritus, gophers, and ragweed.
Now dozers and shovels scrape away
the hills, push through new roads,
a thin carpet of blacktop,
and builders pitch their wooden tents
where trains once sat, where kids
ran free, the last wilderness in town.
There is a plan to put in a park.

Ruining Winter

This time, let's rake the leaves,
the ten thousand maple seeds
helicoptered to the ground.
In this last modest heat of fall, we will work.

Every winter, the blanket of snow
moderates the yard, trapping the beneath,
erasing the undone. Gone/notgone, work
I know needs finished, but don't do.
Come thaw, I'll be on hands and knees,
peeling frozen leaves from yellow grass,
all spring pulling seedling maples
from garden beds, a whole forest
composting with egg shells and potato peels.

I look for the rake, hidden behind a half-built
rabbit hutch. The nails, screws, brads, staples
all need put away. Tools sorted. Scrap wood
scrapped. Another late fall day fades.

The tomatoes ripen yet,
the beans not all gone dead or woody.
There are potatoes and carrots to dig, a last pass
of the mower across shaggy grass.

Let me, for one year, have done what
needed doing, for one year,
to have gotten it right.

The Shepherd Anticipates the Solstice

In the season of fan belts, late in the season
of moss. In the season of whiskey, we light
the fires. We signal to our neighbors across
the long shadows. Our dog-walks, we keep brisk.
our ice-scrapers have wool mittens built-in.
We cover our leaking windows in plastic—the world
becomes a blue blur. The car is on blocks,
the tires removed. Every morning, we check
its progress, inching down the street. Sometimes
it appears to be in the same position
as the night before. But we understand—the pull
of Jupiter is subtle as the first push of spring crocus.
Wrapped around the taproot of every over-wintered
weed, is an earthworm, waiting once more for warmth.

Bridge

Fifteen years ago, a boy was beaten
to death in the alley. Last week, a man
was shot and killed blocks away, his body
run over. Homes have burned both ends
of the street: faulty wiring, meth lab. We
grow Oregon Grape six feet high around
the perimeter of the yard. Across from us,
condos and townhomes rise, new streets
form on top of old. The decay of fall leaves
means fertile soil by spring. Down the road,
a house empties, the cats the man kept
freeze. Winter settles pale as milk. Walking
the alleys is a tunnel of barking dogs, black
labs and pit bull mixes. We keep so much
inside, yards and homes in yellow light.
Stripped-bare shrubs jeweled in ice,
and at last, the work has stopped.
Silence comes with the snow, and down
the steep bank, the river burns on and on.

The Man in the Blue House

He walks the alley, hammer in hand, and taps nails
back into fences. Sometimes he is Dmitri,
sometimes Vanya. Other times, he doesn't know.

He scavenges pallets for the man across the alley,
rebuilds them and piles them in the bed of a pickup.
He accuses ghosts, yells at no one, You can't hide!
another note in the white noise of the neighborhood.

At night he tends a fire of scrap lumber
between his house and the neighbor's garage.
The orange glow lights the alley. Come the winter,
low clouds heavy with snow will glow the same color.

The chickens roost, making small noises back and forth.
A cat is stuck on a roof, yowling hungry all night.
This is how we settle in, October air loose in our mouths.

A Love Poem after Three Years in North Dakota

I want to say this to you.
I've begun many times. I know
a few of the right words
and you listen, I know.
This is years now. Years,
woman-I-love. You see
how tired we are. We make
time into something solid
and palatable. We paint lines
on the flat surface of the world.
We have homes and gardens
and children. We have grown old,
suddenly, in our minds. The hazelnut tree
has matured where you imagined it,
and we pass days gathering
the ripened nuts, cracking them apart
and feasting quietly on what we find within.

Driving West Through Thunderstorms

Only wind screams here. The people
are whispers. The buildings are bad ideas,
but steady. There was no beauty
until I learned to look for it

Clouds over distant plains
dangle rain to spring crops. The hammer
of an oil rig does slow work on the ground,
and what is in the ground.
The landscape of absence grows familiar.

When the clouds break, the birds settle
on new puddles. Another line of clouds follows,
mirrors the basin and range repetition
of the Rocky Mountains.
Eventually, the unbroken Dakota
flatlands give way to the jagged mouth
of Montana. Eventually,
unending clouds give way to unbroken sky.

A Litany of Scars

A simple line under an eye,
or the vast cavity in the face
of Butte, Montana. A record
of things done. This is how we learn
the world. I was young
when Mount St. Helens seared
the Toutle River Valley. I fell down,
running home, and like to think
I can still see the scars on my palms.
Great red slash piles dot the Olympic range,
years old and unburned.

Lani's body—the scar of cancer—
diminished lung capacity
and the bright incision,
stitches parallel on each side.
The red highways of her pregnancy
fade as our children grow,
a map to some older knowledge.
A half-inch scar under Andrea's eye.
A dog—or a zipper, she says. I was young.
On my forehead: chicken-pox.

On the soft clay of memory
there is nothing that can't be recorded.
A man's body remembers his love
for Elizabeth, another, his love for stars.
A scar on my ankle remembers
a bike crash. Lani's lip remembers
the playground carrousel.
Emma's three years of memory
have left no record. The trees remember
falling. St. Helens remembers
three thousand feet of summit.

※　※　※

I wish I had a mark on my body
for each time I've crossed
the Continental Divide on foot,
each time I've made love,
each time a river has been hard
and fast enough to pull me under, smooth rocks
and the current against my body, turning and holding me
far from light.

The Wrecker Finds a Young Hawk Fallen From the Nest

The world is a hard place.
We wait and nothing happens. Nothing
happens and again we wait. Slink back
to some dingy past. Start again, but the same.
An endless loop this bastard world.
When my end comes—
no fruitless turning turning history,
no suffering. Swift and bold.
No shadows. Should I bear you with me?
Everything repeating, hard
world, loop, bastard, bird, time, turn.

Let us leave this rough beast behind.
Silence for silence. Blood rushing
in our ears, over fields, mice scatter,
and you could learn to strike, to soar
to gather heat under your wings.

I could show you what I little know.
My voice fails. In darkness then,
we shall sleep and hush.

You'll Never Be Here Again

or even be able to find it on a map.
And who would want to?
Something so fine could only be
transient. This you know. Of this
you must be certain.

Orange scrim of clouds
bantering the low harvest moon.
You say, Yes, love.
I know already, you can't
mean me, even if once,
you had.

Lonely, we speak past each other
about baseball, the proper way
to hold the bat to lay down
a sacrifice bunt, suicide squeeze,
runner breaking from third
at the pitcher's first move.
Faith pure and love enough
to fling himself down the baseline.

This is what we allow
ourselves. This isn't
white sand and lovers strolling
toward their own deep decay.
Instead, pencil-etched ash
against a fading asphalt sky
and a blanket of dead leaves.

The Nothing Vendor Dream of a Garden

He sang dark moonlight
into her ear, the gourd
alive, leaves unfurling,
unbrellas as spring rain
beckoned the ground.
At the ice-air window
he turns a yard fork.
It leaves him, out the door.
Then hands, brooms,
televisions, old phones.
Soon, the whole
living room, bathroom,
plungers and toilet brushes,
a parade down Broadway.
All the lights are green.
You can see for miles.

Smoking a Cigarette on a Balcony
in Almira, Washington

Light rain. The clouds move from west to east.
Owls in the distance and small birds
scissor and fret. This is the home
I'd longed for. Inside, my lover
is frustrated and beauty.
Outside, the clouds. Outside,
a truck rusts under years of rain
and sun, bales of hay under cover
next to it for horses long since gone. Outside,
a long route back to a place that is no more
home than here. Inside, we make love
in the middle of another day
with nothing else to do. Inside, we wait,
thinking of who waits for us,
for you, we wait. To follow
the road, follow the clouds.
My lover says the clouds here
look different, textures of light
we didn't see in the North Dakota years.
Here's what we did see:
A home that wasn't place. Cold clouds, like us,
only far away for now.

Advanced Practices in Weed Removal

You'll be tempted to yank.

Give thanks to God, even for weeds.

A weed is something that grows
where you don't want it.

Grass is a weed.
Know thine enemy.

'Persistent' and 'pernicious' are terms
often associated with weeds.

The dandelion always wins. So too,
quack grass and mallow.

Don't use gloves or a hand-spade.
You'll get minute spines—
bull thistle, stinging nettle, prickly lettuce—
buried in your hands and arms.
Be not proud.

Gather all the leaves and grip at the soil line.
Your skin will know the way into earth.

You must slide the weed from the ground,
the entire root intact. Leave nothing to sprout later.

You will understand success
when the root releases its
deep grip on the earth with a sigh,
a reluctance to yield
that should be familiar.

※ ※ ※

God knows there are days
you want to salt the soil,
ensure that nothing grows there
ever again.

Hard Wind, End of the Block

He begins with directionless cursing,
a desire to be left alone, unexamined.
He'll do what he goddamn well wants
and you can't fucking stop him.

Maybe you're standing on your porch,
maybe pulling ripe tomatoes from the vine.
Maybe, when you were young, your parents
fought, often and loud. You don't think
about it much anymore. But there are nights
you want to punch through walls,
to take your helplessness by the throat
and crush the life from it.

Right there is where he lives, on that verge.
A hard wind, and no shelter belt to break before.
His anger is a thick barrier around his yard.
After cursing is more cursing and then more.
Neighbors close doors, windows, curtains,
shake their heads, and you do, too.
You've been the small boy, alone in your bed,
listening to the words, the timbre and pitch of them,
the awful music they make. As the wind rises,
your legs shake and you remember learning
that language has power. What need for fists,
in the face of such force? What need for calm,
or peace, or anything but this, for the rest of your life?

What the Sky Lacks

The kayak's bow shears the flat water
a widening vee behind. The paddle
dips left, then right, then stops
and the boat glides on. Mist rises,
the sun an hour from clearing the hills.
Everything I know of sky is ground
reflected in water. What is different
is different, which is nothing,
except clouds the color the expanse
captured here, open elsewhere.

The stretched North Dakota days,
a bright everything that is nothing
but air, a perception of color. Feeling
that changes and has changed. What
the sky lacks is nothing, and this boat
on water is nothing, slicing nothing,
a reflection, the earth and heavens
on the same plane, split by me. The paddle
dips left, then right, then stops
and the boat glides on.

The Nothing Vendor Reflects on the State of the West Central Economy

Transactions are brisk, as ever. This isn't barter, isn't
cap and trade. Cynics might call it theft. But we
are large-hearted, bright-eyed repurposers,
we call our alleys, 'aisles,' and shop with enthusiasm.

A neighbor's fence becomes a compost bin.
Nobody is going to use those 15-inch rims,
but take them if you need them.
The sleeper sofa was made of recyclable metal
and you could use the upholstery for just about anything.
The mattress speaks for itself—it will still make a fine bed,
even after the rain and the cats. Hurry now,
such bargains will end soon.

In time, our economy will slow. Already,
the nonpurposers spill over the near-gated boundaries
of new development. The sign says,
"Spokane's Premier Urban Destination."
A house down the street is bought cheap,
gutted to fit the new economy.

Soon we will chase the repurposers out, build
walls of mown grass, vinyl windows,
and Adirondack chairs. We'll junk our old things,
bus the unowners toward some darker blight,
convert service churches to craft breweries,
wipe our hands and think, how nice,
to have finally cleaned the place up.

The Shepherd Trips over
a Section of Broken Sidewalk

Her attention is drawn, as ever it is, skyward.
Yes, the river, yes, the gnarled old elm trees,
pushing up blocks of concrete. The dogs
have wandered off again. There is no flock
to which the shepherd should attend. Above,
ospreys circle, calling to mates, nested atop
old poles. Sparrows fat on spring bird seed
explode from tree to sky to tree. The shepherd
climbs the steep hill leading out, leaving the hidden
village below. New homes along the new paved trail,
new cars on new streets. But above, the sky is still
the sky. The shepherd avoids a forklift. The men
buildings homes move piles of lumber back and forth,
wonder where it is they'll put all this stuff.

Sam Decides the Fate of the Universe

He was born asking questions
and today he watches a show
about how the world might end.
He sleeps under the sign of giant bat
and tyrannosaur. He dreams loud.
Turning rocks over, he identifies spiders
by color and danger. He collects
dinosaur bones, and pirates, and books.
His Lego city reaches for hazy skies.

    I remember my days, the world
    I laid over this one, the rough roads
    I dug from flower beds, the far universe
    of the alley.

From the couch, he says, with delight
Dad, points at the screen, smiling, eyes wide,
space aliens could wipe us out!

    Later, my mother shows me a picture of me
    at six. She laughs when I ask
    where she got the picture of him.

At bedtime, I find him fending off a dragon
as it attacks Lego city. I stop myself from making
the explosion noises I'd spent a youth perfecting.
He's perfecting his own. And if we all live
in his imagined world, I'm content
we'll be safe a while longer yet.

This is the Stuff I am Selling

Clear morning grays
to threaten rain, clouds
a storm of geese
and across the river
more new homes.

For sale: sterling silver we used
at Thanksgiving the year
Marshall decided against
the cranberry sauce.

A puppet theatre—no, I'm sorry,
the children kept the puppets.

This camera I used
to take her picture,
nude and laughing,
in the creek-lit shine
of a morning like this,
and there's the book I wrote
on how to love her, called,
Hold Fast.

The geese have turned to bees,
and the new homes have sprouted
wings. They buzz.

You're just driving by, but
let me tempt you
with this BBQ spatula, or this dryer.
It needs a new belt.

For sale: one oak table,
only made love upon twice. Sturdy.

Please, no charge for the Coleman stove,
the toasting glasses we bought in Austria.

Her clothes hung on those hangers—
take them, and this picture of bees.
The chair and the toys,
suitcases, one hard-shelled, one
with a broken wheel. Take the shoes
I am wearing, and my glasses.

Even the lawn is flying away.
I'll make you a bargain
on the soil that remains.

Having Once Lived in North Dakota

There were long days
when nothing seemed wrong.
Sedate wind at Turtle River
and midstream fishing for the one
hatchery trout with an appetite
for corn. The sun closed down
the sky and night mouthed warmth
into the ear of distant winter.
Children played late, adults later,
banking the heat, the whole immense sky,
against the deficiency of light October meant,
the farmers frantic in planting and reaping.
The dream was always there—
cracked cold, guttural winter,
the flood season to follow.

Notes and Acknowledgements

"Dream of the Wrecker" is a glosa, borrowing the first line of each stanza from Christopher Howell's poem, "Today" (*Light's Ladder.* U Washington P, 2004).

"North Dakota" is an imitation of Paul Éluard's "L'Amoreuse" (*The Selected Writings of Paul Eluard.* New Directions, 1952).

"A Siege of Cranes" was written with Jennifer Reid. We alternated lines via text message, revising cooperatively.

The following poems appeared in the chapbook, *A Visitor's Guide to North Dakota,* published in 2007 by Finishing Line Press: "Eastbound on the Empire Builder"; "Closing the Blue Spark"; "A Visitor's Guide to North Dakota"; "Then Snow"; "Uncertain Daylight"; "The Last Remaining Light"; "Failure of Imagination"; "End/Beginning"; "Hunting the Mitchell Property"; "Where the Trees Begin, Where the Trees End"; "Driving West Through Thunderstorms"; and "Certain Knowledge."

Thanks to the following journals for publishing poems from this collection:

Ascent: "The Man in the Blue House"
Isthmus: "Having Once Lived in North Dakota"
New South: "Under Sheltering Trees My Daughter and I Consider the Coming Storm"
Railtown Almanac: a Spokane poetry anthology: "The Roadside Nothing Vendor"; "Last Wild"
Redactions: "Language Acquisition"; "The Nothing Vendor Reflects on the State of the West Central Economy"
Red Rock Review: "What was Once Comfort" as "Uncertain Daylight"; "The Dream of the Wrecker"; "Hunting the Mitchell Property"

Relief: "Naming the Spiders"; "Advanced Practices in Weed Removal"

Ruminate: "You'll Never Be Here Again"

Smartish Pace: "An Unfinished Sky"

The Spokesman-Review. "The Shepherd Anticipates the Solstice"; "Bridge"

Sugar House Review: "This is the Stuff I am Selling"

The Swamp: "Hard Wind, End of the Block"

Talking River: "Field Dressing"; "A Litany of Scars"; "How to Hunt Badly"

Theopoetics: "The Names of Things We've Lost"; "What the Sky Lacks"

Town Creek Poetry: "When I Could, and then Couldn't, and then the Moon"

Yalobusha Review: "On the Westbound Train"

Special thanks to the Spokane Arts Fund, the City of Spokane, Spokane Public Libraries and the Spokane County Library Districts. Also, to Spokane Poetry Slam, my fellow Chickenheads: Jeffrey G. Dodd, Kathryn Smith, and Ellen Welcker. To all the residents of the Commune, past, present, and future, to the shepherd-who-watches-over-us, and as ever, to Lani.

Thom Caraway teaches at Whitworth University in Spokane, Washington, where he is the editor of *Rock & Sling*, a journal of witness. His work has been published in *Sugar House Review, Smartish Pace, North Dakota Quarterly, Ruminate, Relief,* and elsewhere. Thom was also named Spokane's first Poet Laureate, which came with many fewer free drinks than he'd anticipated, but many more great friends. He is also a regular designer of things generally bookish and sometimes arty. He is the founding Editor of Sage Hill Press, Spokane's longest-running independent small press. He generally appreciates bold display type and sans serifs of all origins.

Titles in this volume are set in Mrs. Eaves, designed originally as a display type by Zuzana Licko in 1996. The face is itself an adaptation of Baskerville, whose designer married Sarah Eaves after her husband left her with five children and later died. Eaves eventually became an instrumental assistant to Baskerville's typesetting and printing. In Licko's words, Mrs. Eaves is "just enough tradition with an updated twist."

Body text is arranged in Franklin Gothic Book. Named in honor of Benjamin Franklin, Franklin Gothic was originally designed by American type designer Morris Fuller Benton, head designer of American Type Founders from 1900-1937. The typeface was endlessly adapted and extended throughout the twentieth century, including several ITC versions created by Victor Caruso in the 1970s. The face used here is based on Caruso's monotype ITC version of Franklin Gothic Book.

Made in the USA
Middletown, DE
27 June 2019